You Don't Have to Be Sick to Get Better!

You Don't Have to Be Sick to Get Better!

Thoughts on Living a Better Life and Being a Better Person

Michael Josephson

Joseph and Edna Josephson Institute of Ethics
Marina del Rey, California

2001

Published by the Josephson Institute of Ethics
Marina del Rey, California
Copyright ©2001 by Michael Josephson

All rights reserved under International and Pan-American
Copyright Conventions. Published in the United States by the
Josephson Institute.

www.charactercounts.org / www.josephsoninstitute.org

CHARACTER COUNTS! is a service mark of the CHARACTER
COUNTS! Coalition, a project of the Josephson Institute.

ISBN 1-888689-12-9

Publisher's Cataloging-in-Publication
(Provided by Quality Books, Inc.)

Josephson, Michael (Michael S.), 1942-
    You don't have to be sick to get better! : thoughts
  on living a better life and being a better person /
  Michael Josephson. -- 1st ed.
    p. cm.
    ISBN 1-888689-12-9

    1. Ethics. 2. Character.   I. Title.

BJ1012.J67 2001   171
                         QBI33-175

Manufactured in the United States of America
First Edition

Contents

Acknowledgments

First, I must acknowledge the ultimate inspiration for all my best thoughts contained in this book: my parents Joseph and Edna, my wife Anne, whose insights and patience both stimulate and support me, and my five magnificent children: Justin, Samara, Abrielle, Carissa and Mataya.

Second, I have to thank Bob Sims of KNX radio in Los Angeles for the idea of creating these radio commentaries and for his confidence and support in airing them three times a day during valuable "drive time."

Finally, I want to acknowledge and thank all the people of the Josephson Institute team who have played vital roles in the production of the radio commentaries and its translation into this book. Very special thanks to Lauren Fair, my administrative assistant who expands my capacity tenfold; to Tom DeCair, who has organized and administered the commentaries and our relationships with KNX and other radio stations carrying them; to Terry Harrison, who selected, edited and organized the commentaries in this volume; to Wes Hanson, who designed the cover and page layout and has overseen the entire editing and publishing effort; to John Auld, a longtime friend and adviser whose company, Pace Publications in Anaheim, CA, printed this book; to Steve Nish, who has kept the commentaries accessible in text and audio form on our web page (www.charactercounts.org); to Todd Katzberg, who organizes and sends out our weekly e-mail of the commentaries; to Dan McNeill, who with Steve and Todd provided crucial editing services; to Cory Izquierdo, who responds to inquiries about the commentaries; and to Marjorie Tibar and Ed Uyehara, who manage the complex data collection and distribution of our growing list of subscribers. — *MSJ*

Introduction

Nearly five years ago I received a call from Bob Sims, program manager of KNX-1070 AM, a CBS all-news station in Los Angeles. He asked if I'd be interested in creating a daily 90-second commentary discussing issues of ethics and character.

I was initially horrified at the idea of taking on another project, especially one as challenging as composing daily essays to be inserted between news and traffic reports. I was then, as I am now, a full-time volunteer at the Joseph and Edna Josephson Institute of Ethics, a nonprofit organization I founded in honor of my parents in 1987.

Bob said he didn't know if these commentaries would find an audience but it was worth a try and, as the ultimate lure, he said I could write about anything I wanted. The temptation was too great to resist. I had always wanted to be a stand-up philosopher, and this was one of the biggest public platforms in Southern California.

Writing hopefully cogent essays in 300 words or less was a much tougher challenge than I imagined, and I developed the awful habit of writing most of them between 10:00 PM and 4:00 AM after the rest of my day was done. I'd then have a messenger pick them up so they would air at 6:55 AM. I never dreamed the series would catch on and that preparing these daily commentaries would become a central part of my professional life.

As requests for written transcripts of individual commentaries started to mount, the Institute began sending weekly e-mails of the commentaries at no charge. Within a few months the subscription list grew to about 20,000 (you can subscribe at www.charactercounts.org), and people began to suggest collecting selected commentaries into a book suitable for gifts. That is what you have here.

Looking back at how I got to this wonderful place fills me with surprise. For one thing, I

30. At the same time, we were emphatically "nonjudgmental" on matters of personal morality, and I bought into the do-your-own-thing morality of the times. Probably my strongest ethical conviction in those days was: "It's wrong to be judgmental." Issues of right and wrong were intensely personal. "Whatever feels right for you is right for you."

Immediately after graduating law school I took a position on the faculty of the University of Michigan Law School. I fell in love with teaching, which has been my occupation and avocation ever since. During my years as a law professor I also became a bit of an entrepreneur. I created a company that published study aids for law students and helped law school graduates prepare for the bar examination.

The turning point from the theory and gamesmanship of law and lawyering began in 1976, several years after I joined the faculty at Loyola Law School in Los Angeles. That year I was assigned to teach the course in legal ethics. You see, shortly after the Watergate scandal (which involved no less than 20 lawyers), the

American Bar Association fretted: "Where did we go wrong?" Someone came up with the explanation: "They didn't have a course in ethics." Right. How would lawyers know not to lie without a course in ethics?

Anyway, the bar association mandated that every law school offer a required course in ethics, and deans had to assign faculty to teach the course. When my turn came, I was not enthusiastic. I read, for the first time, the lawyer's Code of Professional Responsibility and looked for loopholes and ambiguities. The idea that ethics was a subject of real substance and importance only began to take root as the result of a very personal experience that coincided with my new teaching assignment. I became a father for the first time — on Lincoln's birthday in 1976 with the birth of my son Justin. As the months rolled by, I became increasingly conscious of the awesome moral responsibilities of fatherhood.

I would never again look at issues of right and wrong with detached intellectual neutrality. I was surprised to see how quickly I shed my nonjudgmental ethical relativism. It mattered very much what kind of person Justin would be. How could I be sure he would become a man of character and integrity when there was so much I did not know or understand about the nature of ethics and morality? One thing was clear, though: Looking at life purely in terms of costs and benefits, risks and rewards, as I had been doing as a law professor, simply wouldn't cut it.

Though I never wanted the responsibility of being a role model, I had no choice. From then on, what I said, what I did, what I demanded and what I permitted would take on a special importance because I was a father. Unfortunately, recognition of my new responsibilities was not enough to endow me with special moral wisdom to know what was right. Nor did it give me the strength of character to always do what I knew I should do. A great deal of self-reflection and study was ahead of me.

In 1985, I sold my company for a great deal of money. This allowed me to donate the start-up funds to establish the Joseph & Edna Josephson Institute of Ethics, a nonprofit organization named in honor of my parents. In 1987,

I gave up my law school tenure and began to serve as a full-time volunteer CEO, lecturer and writer trying to improve the ethical quality of personal and organizational behavior.

Although I have been a full-time ethicist since 1987, I haven't found all the answers. In fact, I still struggle with basic issues of honesty, respect, responsibility and fairness in my own life. I must fight my tendency to exaggerate when I am promoting the work of the Institute, to make false excuses when I fall short on my commitments, and to use my verbal skills to manipulate or injure people. I often have to remind myself to be more generous about mental or moral frailties in myself and others, and to be more kind, sensitive and appreciative, especially to those whose love or friendship I take for granted. As an employer, I frequently battle with discomfort and uncertainty trying to balance my sense of duty to efficiency against concepts of caring and kindness, especially when I make decisions about salary, promotion or termination. And, as someone with the financial resources to help family, friends and charitable organizations, I have huge doubts about what is right and fair, about how much is enough, or when I should say no.

When I was offered a lot of money for the company I had been running on the side, I recognized that I had an extraordinary opportunity to choose what I wanted to do with the rest of my life. Someone once said, "If you want to know how to live your life, think about what you want people to say about you after you die and live backward." When I realized that I was unconsciously writing my epitaph with hundreds of little decisions and deeds, it became more important to make sound principled decisions worthy of my highest moral aspirations.

Though both my parents are gone, I have a wonderful wife, Anne, and five incredible children (Justin, 25; Samara, 8; Abrielle, 6; Carissa 5; and Mataya, 3). More than ever, I feel a sense of opportunity and obligation to live my life in a way that will be worthy of their pride and admiration and to use whatever teaching skills I have to make a positive difference in the world.

The cover of this volume symbolizes a powerful story that helps drive my efforts. It's about a young boy who came upon a beach scattered with starfish that had washed up on the sand. They had been abandoned by a rapidly receding tide and would surely die if they could not get back to the water. The boy was beginning to pick them up and throw them into the ocean one by one when an old fellow challenged him. "What are you doing?" he demanded. "I'm saving these starfish," the boy answered. The old man huffed, "There are hundreds of them out here and most are probably already dead. What you're doing won't make any difference." The boy held one living creature in his hand and said, "It makes a difference to this starfish." And he threw it in the water.

We change the world and ourselves one starfish at a time. What we do does make a difference.

— *Michael Josephson*
Los Angeles, California
November 2001

Character *Does* Count

Character is fate.

Heraclitus

You Don't Have to Be Sick to Get Better

As a full-time ethicist — can you believe there even is such a thing? — I spend lots of time talking about right and wrong with parents and politicians, kids and corporate managers, journalists and generals.

One thing I have learned is that while most people have a high self-image when it comes to ethics, being a good person and doing the right thing are easier said than done. For one thing, it's not always easy knowing what's right. If I was supposed to have learned everything I needed to know about ethics in kindergarten, I must have been absent that day. Second, having the moral willpower to put ethical principles above self-interest and always do the right thing takes a lot of character, especially when no one else seems to be living up to such high standards.

The fact is that for most of us, trying to live a good life engages us in a constant struggle between what we want to do (our desires) and what we should do (our ethical duties). Even basically good people may lie occasionally, cheat just a little and rationalize away moral compromises. It's human nature. No one is perfect.

But it's also human nature to strive for perfection and to care about our character. When it comes to ethics, you don't have to be sick to get better. And getting better is important if we want to improve the quality of our lives and set the example we should for our children.

The True Meaning of Our Lives

I saw a cartoon of an old king checking in at the gates of heaven. The gatekeeper, with a large book in front of him, said, "Edward the Good, huh? Well, Eddie, we will be the judge of that." The point is that, in the end, generous self-appraisals won't matter. Our epitaphs will be written and eulogies delivered by the people who knew how we lived. The real meaning of our lives may be defined by how we are remembered.

When a Swedish newspaper printed Alfred Nobel's obituary by mistake, he had the rare opportunity to see how others saw him. It changed his life dramatically. Though the article was complimentary, describing Mr. Nobel as a brilliant chemist who made a great fortune as the inventor of dynamite, he was horrified to be memorialized in such materialistic terms. Determined to leave a more positive legacy, he bequeathed his considerable wealth to the establishment of the Nobel Prizes to acknowledge great human achievements. Few of us can create something as momentous as the Nobel Prizes, but we can all live lives that earn a eulogy our children and parents would be proud of.

In the hurly-burly of everyday living it's hard to keep perspective. Money, position, pride and power seem so important — until they're not. At the end of their lives, no one says, "I wish I spent more time at the office." It's a matter of priorities.

So if you want to know how to live your life, just think about what you want people to say about you after you die and live backwards.

Bart and the Flood

Bart was caught in a flood. The water was a foot high when a rescue truck offered to help him evacuate. Bart refused, saying, "God will provide." When the levee broke, he had to climb onto the roof. A man in a rowboat came by and urged him to get aboard. But again Bart refused: "God will provide." The waters rose so high that Bart had to climb to the top of the chimney and eventually the water swept him away. As a helicopter pilot was maneuvering to rescue him, Bart yelled to the sky, "God, why have you forsaken me?"

The pilot yelled back, "God didn't forsake you. He sent you a truck, then a boat, and now this helicopter. Now, use the arms he gave you to grab this rope."

Not only our survival, but also our happiness depends on our ability to discover and use the resources we have. That's the timeless message of *The Wizard of Oz*: the Scarecrow, Tin Man and Lion already had the qualities they sought from the Wizard. They just didn't know it.

In our personal lives and in the workplace, we tend to focus on what we think we need rather than mustering up the power and strength we already have to make our lives better. Most of us greatly underestimate and underuse the power within us to make our lives better. For some the obstacle is fear, for others laziness, and still others are immobilized by their own pessimism. Wanting, wishing and worrying waste psychic energy. They are useful only if they are a prelude to a planned course of action, including the willingness to work, and wait, for what we want. As a famous golfer once said, "It's amazing. The harder I practice, the luckier I get."

The Woodsman and the Leprechaun

Long ago, a woodsman saved the life of a leprechaun and was given one wish. The woodsman thought for a long time and finally wished that each of his three daughters find a good husband.

But the leprechaun was full of games: "How am I to know what's good in your mind? I'll give them husbands, but you can name only one quality and it's got to be the same for all. What'll you have? Wealth, fame, intelligence, beauty... you name it."

The woodsman thought again. "Give me men of good character, then."

The leprechaun wasn't done playing. "And how am I to know what good character is?" he asked.

"Do you have children?" the woodsman countered.

"I do."

"And do you love them?"

"More than life itself."

"Then give my girls the kind of men you want for your children."

"Ah," the leprechaun said, "then you shall have honorable men with kind and loving hearts. And I'll throw in a strong conscience too."

What would you have chosen? Sure, wealth can buy a lot of pleasures. And intelligence, fame and beauty are great assets that can make life more enjoyable. But through the lens of parental love, the importance of good character stands out. I call this the parent perspective, a worldview that defines good character with clarity and provides a powerful impetus for our own morality. Next time you face an ethical temptation or dilemma just ask yourself what you hope your children and the people they date and marry would do. Or what action would best earn their pride and make the world the kind of world you want your children to live in.

Admitting Errors

As several listeners pointed out, I once made a broadcast mistake when I attributed the Army's slogan: "Be all that you can be," to the Marine Corps. I apologized to all concerned. It was a foolish error.

It's a lot easier now for me to admit when I'm wrong than it was earlier in my career. A turning point occurred during my third year of teaching law while I was still the youngest professor at my law school. During one of my classes, after I explained a particular statute, a student suggested that I had misinterpreted the law. In fact, he said, it meant the opposite of what I said. I read the provision again and it was immediately apparent that he was right. More crucially, I was wrong.

My immediate reaction was to confuse the issue and bluff my way through. But I realized that if I failed to fess up, I'd be sending more than 100 soon-to-be lawyers into the world with dangerous misinformation. I remember the sinking feeling that my academic career was about to be nipped in the bud. Though I thought the earth would open up and swallow me, I was surprised that my disclosure simply produced some murmurs and frantic note-taking.

Still, I was mortified and as soon as the class ended I darted for the exit. To my horror, the student who corrected me cut off my escape. I was ready for the worst when he said, "Professor Josephson, I want to thank you. This was the first time I ever saw a teacher admit he was wrong. It was great." Thanks to this gracious student, I not only survived my first public error (there were many more to follow), but I learned that admitting a mistake can actually build credibility. I think of this every time I see someone squirming shamefully to cover up rather than confess an error.

The Basic Tenets of
CHARACTER COUNTS!

Since National **CHARACTER COUNTS!** Week is the third week of October, I'm sure you want to review the basic tenets of **CHARACTER COUNTS!** so you'll be ready when the time comes. You never know when someone is going to test you. After all, it's a growing program that has already been embraced by hundreds of organizations, including the YMCA, AYSO, Boys and Girls Clubs, Big Brothers Big Sisters and educational organizations like the American Federation of Teachers and the National Education Association.

CHARACTER COUNTS! is based on the idea that character development is, first and foremost, the obligation of families, but that conscientious efforts by schools, youth-development, civic and religious organizations play a crucial role in fostering good character based on shared ethical values.

These values, called the "Six Pillars of Character," define the essence of good character in terms that are acceptable to liberals and conservatives, the religious and the secular. Invoking these shared values, Congress, the president and more than 500 communities have proclaimed **CHARACTER COUNTS!** Week (the third week of October).

Here are the "Six Pillars of Character": trustworthiness, respect, responsibility, fairness, caring and citizenship. Trustworthiness embraces four essential traits: integrity, honesty, promise-keeping and loyalty. Respect requires us to recognize the worth and dignity of others and live by the Golden Rule. Responsibility includes the ideas of duty, self-control and accountability. Fairness is about justice, openness and consistency. Caring refers to qualities of kindness, compassion and charity. And citizenship is about being a good neighbor, doing one's share and protecting the environment. **CHARACTER COUNTS!** is about developing all these characteristics — a daunting task.

Give Her Whatever You Want

Ken Lloyd, author of *Jerks at Work: How to Deal With People Problems and Problem People*, sent me a parable I'd like to share. It's about two partners in the old country who went on a business trip. They worked hard and amassed 200 pieces of gold. As they were about to head home, one of them became fatally ill. As he was dying, he told his partner, "Give my wife whatever you want."

When the survivor returned to his village he told his partner's wife of her husband's death and he gave her one piece of gold. She objected, but the partner said, "I am simply carrying out your husband's last wishes." The wife could not figure out what her husband has been thinking, but she knew he was a smart and ethical man, so she suggested that they go to a village judge. The business partner, knowing the judge's reputation for strictly following the law, agreed. After the judge heard the story he awarded 199 pieces of gold to the wife.

The shocked partner protested: "How can you ignore the words of a dying man asking me to give his wife whatever I want?" The judge said, "I'm applying his words precisely. You obviously want 199 pieces of gold and that's exactly what you should give his wife."

There are a couple of lessons from this story. First, it's clear how treacherous it is when we set aside simple notions of justice and rely on technical, literal interpretations of law. Narrow legalism is often a double-edged sword that can cut either party in unanticipated ways. Second, it reminds us how self-destructive greed can be and that fairness is not something to worry about only when we have to. It's a fundamental moral virtue that guides the behavior of people of honor.

Duty to Myself: A Euphemism for Selfishness

I was presenting the view that living a good life as a person of character involved giving up some of the things we want to meet our ethical duties. As the conversation turned to the issue of balancing family obligations and career goals, someone asked, "What about my duty to myself?"

The idea that we not only have a right to pursue personal happiness but a duty to do so has shaped modern culture since the 60s. Thus, being happy, fulfilled and actualized came to be treated as a moral obligation to respect our own feelings and be honest, loving and fair to ourselves.

Sure, in making life's trade-offs it's important to remember that our happiness counts too, but to elevate this to a duty troubles me. When we think of looking out for our own interests as a duty, it legitimizes a self-absorbed worldview that puts personal desires for happiness, freedom and pleasure on equal footing with our ethical responsibilities to others. Inevitably, people preoccupied with the counterfeit idea of duty to self end up ignoring authentic moral duties to parents, children, friends and employers.

This rationalized form of selfishness provides the philosophical basis for much of the self-indulgent, unethical behavior in society today. It's a primary cause of an "I deserve it" attitude that translates to the creed: Whatever I want, I need; whatever I need I have a right to have.

Ethics doesn't require us to ignore self-interest. It doesn't demand a life full of self-sacrifice. But it does require that we know the difference between what we want and what we should do and that we live according to basic moral principles requiring us to be honest, respectful, kind and responsible.

I'm Emma: A Story of Self-Control

A frazzled mother entered a grocery store with a crying child. "Emma," she said, "you can do this. We just have to get a few things." Moments later, the child became more upset and the woman said calmly, "It's OK, Emma. Just a couple more items." When the child became hysterical in the checkout line the mom took a deep breath and said, "Emma, hold it together. We'll be in the car in a few minutes." In the parking lot a woman stopped her. "Excuse me, I couldn't help but notice you in the store and I just wanted to compliment you on how patient you are with little Emma." The mother laughed. "Well thank you, but the truth is, I'm Emma."

Self-control is a virtue that doesn't come easily. This mother had to work on it, talking herself through each challenge. According to Dr. Daniel Goleman in his book *Emotional Intelligence*, controlling impulses like frustration and anger is a crucial aspect of character. In fact, he says, "Those who are at the mercy of impulse — who lack self-control — suffer a moral deficiency."

Today, many people elevate self-indulgence over self-control. Some indulge angry feelings and let them emerge in harmful words and acts. Others ruin their lives and pollute their environment by indulging emotions like spite, hatred, prejudice, jealousy, negativism and cynicism. Rather than starve these negative sentiments with inattention, they feed them with continual thought and talk.

Controlling our attitudes is not easy. It takes character to harness powerful and instinctive feelings and redirect our thoughts toward positive attitudes, but those who do live happier lives in a happier world.

A Check For the Full Amount

S am called his three closest friends to his deathbed to make a final wish. He said he would give each of them $20,000, but they had to promise to put it in his coffin after he died so he'd have spending money for the afterlife.

They tried to talk him out of it, telling him there would be no use for cash in an afterlife, but Sam was unbending. From his perspective there was no downside. In the end, they made the promise and took the money.

At the funeral each friend put an envelope in the coffin, but as they exited one confessed, "I didn't put all the money in the envelope. I took out $5,000 to give to the poor."

You Don't Have to Be Sick to Get Better!

The second friend looked relieved. "I didn't put in all the money either. You know I was Sam's accountant. I put his estate in order, but I never had a chance to bill him. I just took out the $10,000 he owed me."

The third friend was outraged, declaring: "He was our friend and we made solemn promises. *My* word is my bond. That's why I gave him a check for the full amount."

In fact, all three friends broke a promise, but none of them felt guilty because they rationalized. One did it for a greater good, another under a claim of right and the third masked his greedy intentions with a legalistic illusion that it wasn't his responsibility if Sam couldn't cash the check.

In your pursuit of moral excellence, remember how easy it is to bridge the gap between what we want to do and what we should do with a rationalization.

The Golden Rule

"**D**o unto others as you would have them do unto you."

The Golden Rule is an ethical principle rooted in every major culture. You can find it in the writings of Confucius and Aristotle as well as in the scriptures of virtually all religions. You don't want to be lied to, yelled at or treated unfairly, so don't lie to, yell at or be unfair to others.

It's a terrific rule to create a more kind and just society, and it is central to the ethical principle of respect. But if we're not careful, we can twist the meaning of the Golden Rule by treating it as a rule of exchange rather than a rule of ethics. In other words, we are honest, kind or fair to others only so they will be honest, kind and fair to us.

There is, of course, a practical aspect to the Golden Rule. Kindness often begets kindness, and people are more likely to be honest with us if we're honest with them. The trouble is that if we anchor our willingness to treat others well in expectation that they will return the favor, what is our moral duty with respect to selfish, disrespectful and dishonest people? Can we modify the rule to "Do unto others as they have done unto us," or "before they do it to us?"

Is it ethical to lie to a liar or cheat a cheater? Not for a person of character. We may feel like suckers from time to time if we're honest and kind to everyone, but in the end the best reason to follow the Golden Rule is not because it assures us that others will treat us right, but because it *is* right. You see, how we treat others is not simply about them. It's about us. It defines who we are.

Being Basically Honest

After a workshop, a fellow said, "I don't always play by the rules or tell the truth and some of the things you said made me a little uncomfortable. But I realized I'm 'basically' honest. Isn't that enough?" I don't think so.

What does it really mean when someone declares that they're "basically honest"? I think it means that they are willing to be honest unless it costs too much. They're willing to be honest as long as they get what they want. In the end, I think it means "being honest enough." It reminds me of a cartoon where one man is talking about another: "I admire honesty, but his insistence on being scrupulously honest is really annoying."

People who are content being basically honest are admitting that, when the stakes are high enough, they're willing to be dishonest. Doesn't that mean they're basically dishonest?

After all, how many times do you get to lie before you are a liar? How many times does someone get to lie to you before distrust sets in? A former presidential press secretary told a university audience that he believed in always telling the truth to the press. "That way," he said, "they will believe you when you have to lie." Honesty isn't just an illusion created for public relations. The best liars rarely lie. That's the secret of their success. They may be basically honest, but they're not trustworthy.

Michael Josephson

Even Frogs Need Encouragement

A group of frogs was traveling through the woods and two of them fell into a deep pit. All the other frogs gathered around the pit and watched as the imprisoned frogs tried to jump out. The frogs on top could see there was no way out and they started yelling at the frogs to give up. "The pit is too deep. You're as good as dead," the chorus said.

When the trapped frogs kept trying, the crowd yelled louder, "Give up! You're as good as dead!"

After awhile one of the exhausted frogs heeded what the others were saying, and he fell down and died.

But the second frog kept jumping as hard as she could despite the hopelessness conveyed by those who kept yelling at her to accept the inevitable and just die. Finally, with one valiant jump, she made it out of the pit.

You see, this frog was deaf and unable to hear what the others were saying. She thought they were encouraging her the entire time. And that made all the difference.

A woman named Patty, who was homeless for a long time before she became a resident of a Santa Monica transitional housing program, gave a copy of this story to my wife. Patty understood the moral of this parable all too well and she wanted my wife to understand how powerful words can be to people who are down. While negative words can kill the spirit and the will to fight, encouraging words can help the down-and-out become the up-and-out. Patty said she got out of her own deep pit because caring people at this housing program gave her the faith and confidence she needed to jump a little harder.

Michael Josephson

Character at Home

Be happy. Talk happiness. Happiness calls out responsive gladness in others. There is enough sadness in the world without yours…. Resolve to keep happy and your joy and you shall form an invicible host against difficulties.

Helen Keller

Abrielle Meets Mr. Trouble

I was at a YMCA soccer game watching my oldest daughter play for the Fast Green Tigers and I got a glimpse of the future. And I didn't like it. My then three-year-old, Abrielle, picked out a boyfriend. And who does she go for? An older kid named Brennan. He was nearly four and he had trouble written all over him. Actually, his shirt said, "Member of the Permanent Time-Out Club." This was no fluke. The week before his shirt said, "I didn't do it. If I did, you can't prove it. I want to speak to my lawyer." That's right, he was a kid with a warning label.

And sure enough, in no time my sweet Abrielle followed this pied piper of mischief into an enclosed area behind a shed. There was a gap in a chainlink fence that only a child could slip through. Then he began throwing rocks. It's a father's nightmare. Your daughter picks a fella and all the good sense you taught her goes out the window.

I tracked her down, told her the situation wasn't safe and asked her to come out. But the seeds of "this is my life" rebellion were already sown. She argued with me and I had to sweet-talk her out. I patiently explained to Abrielle it wasn't safe. She seemed convinced, but minutes later I saw her try to get Brennan to reform. She said it wasn't safe. He said he didn't care. She looked to see if I was watching, and she slipped back in, Bonnie joining Clyde in a life of crime. It was harder getting her out this time. I left dreading the time when nothing that I say will overcome the power of her own instincts. I resolved to intensify my work on her character — and Brennan's.

A Promise
Is a Promise

One of the little sayings we have at my house is, "A promise is a promise." It's meant to emphasize that a promise is a very special kind of commitment that needs to be kept — it's part of being trustworthy. So I try to be careful about saying anything to the Josephson girls — my wife and four daughters — that can be construed as a promise. But sometimes I'm careless.

While making breakfast for my then six-year-old daughter Samara, I put a small powdered doughnut on top of her Froot Loops. That may sound gross to you, but she was thrilled. I was making amends for working late the night before and not being home to put her to bed. Moments later, I heard a scream of anguish. Her then two-year-old sister had taken the doughnut and stuffed it into her mouth.

Thinking I had more in the kitchen, I pledged to get her another doughnut. In fact, in a blatant effort to bribe her, I promised two doughnuts. I didn't know the two-year-old had found and squished my whole supply. "Will you go to the store and get some more?" Samara said sweetly.

Realizing I had to leave for work, I tried to finesse the situation: "Sure, angel, I'll bring you doughnuts tonight."

"No," she said looking me directly in the eye. "You promised!" I shamelessly raised the bribe to a whole box of doughnuts if she'd let me off the hook. With tears in her eyes, she said, "A promise is a promise."

I was trapped. I jumped into the car, went to a nearby convenience store, bought a box of doughnuts and returned to meet my commitment. The whole transaction took about 18 minutes. It was worth it. When she hugged me, I whispered, "A promise is a promise."

Can I Borrow $125?

Martin was disappointed that his father didn't attend the last soccer game of the season, but he wasn't surprised. They had talked about it. Martin was a mature 10-year-old; he understood that his father was a very important attorney who worked most weekends. Still, he knew he was loved because, even though his dad often seemed distracted or exhausted, he always asked Martin about the game, hugged him and said he was proud.

Later that evening, Martin interrupted his father's work to ask him how much lawyers make per hour. Annoyed, the father tried to evade the question, but Martin persisted and he was finally told, "Well, son, I charge $200 per hour." Martin gasped and asked if he could borrow $125. Now the father became really irritated. He said no and told his son to go to bed.

Feeling guilty, the father went to Martin's room to find his son sobbing. "Son, you've never asked for money before and you must have a good reason. I'm going to give it to you, but can I ask why you want it?"

The boy's face brightened. "Well, with the $75 I've saved I now have enough."

"Enough for what?"

"Daddy, would you sell me an hour of your time so you can come to the awards banquet on Friday?"

Like Martin's father, many modern parents face a very difficult challenge: trying to find a healthy and proper balance between the insatiable demands of their jobs and the needs of their families. Most overworked parents are not uncaring or neglectful. They're simply stretched to their limit and doing the best they can. Still, the issue is one of priorities, and it never goes away. No one really knows how much is enough, but if we don't arrange our lives to be there for our children, they will regret it — and after it's too late, so will we.

Michael Josephson

Dealing With Growing Older

I had just been through an intense few days full of highs and lows. On the high side were two simple but significant milestones: the seventh birthday of our eldest daughter and early indications that our youngest was well on her way to diaper independence. Sandwiched between these cheerful plateaus of childhood were two other events that cast a more somber light on the process of growing older: a visit to an emergency veterinary hospital for our dog, Lincoln, and the fortieth reunion of my Westchester High School class.

The visit to the vet confirmed that Lincoln's problems, including painful progressive arthritis, were simply signs of age and an unwelcome reminder that we would soon have to help our four young daughters understand and deal with their friend's failing health and inevitable death.

The reunion with former classmates, who looked shockingly like their own parents and grandparents, was even more sobering. I can count birthdays and I know that both my youth and middle age are behind me, but nothing emphasizes the inescapable hazards of aging more dramatically than seeing a growing list of contemporaries who have passed away. When our friends begin to die, we tend to face our own mortality, and think more about what we will leave behind and what, if anything, we can do to prepare those who love us for our own ultimate departure.

My perspective is not one of morbid fear or depression but of attentiveness. The idea is not to think more about death, but about life and how to best spend our time. Viktor Frankl wrote in *Man's Search for Meaning* that one of the strongest antidotes to suicidal feelings is the belief that there is still something to do. So, if we want to live longer and more fully we should be sure to have plenty to do. Plan as if we're going to live forever and live as if we will die tomorrow.

Dealing With Post-Holiday Distress Syndrome

I needed help. I was suffering from PHD syndrome. No, it doesn't have anything to do with dealing with people with doctorate degrees. I'm referring to Post-Holiday Distress.

Don't get me wrong. The recent holidays offered lots of great moments with my five children — including four little girls then six and under. But I have to confess, it's increasingly hard for me to deal with the avalanche of toys and other goodies that seem to bury my non-materialistic values. As worthy and wonderful as my kids are, I can't shake the guilty feeling that they simply have too many things and that the seemingly endless supply of presents will ultimately distort their values with unhealthy expectations and dilute their ability to truly enjoy gifts.

The holidays also wore me out with their mind-numbing cycle of packing, wrapping, unwrapping and disposing of the packings and wrappings. It wasn't just my Scrooge-like sense of waste concerning the expensive but hardly noticed wrapping paper ripped off in seconds. The process of opening the packages literally brought me to my knees.

The sweet, "Will you open my doll, Daddy?" turned into a mental and physical ordeal that revealed flaws in my character. Have you tried to remove a Barbie doll from her cardboard and plastic prison lately? You need an array of tools, and great patience. Having neither, I resorted to brute strength to rip through outer packaging apparently designed to withstand an asteroid storm. Then I was faced with the more daunting challenge of finding and removing all the wire that secures the toy to a cardboard backing. Then, of course, was the issue of batteries. It's not enough to keep a substantial stock of nine -volt, D- cell, C- cell, double-A and triple-A batteries. Now you need a tiny Phillips-head screwdriver to get the batteries in. Do you think there's a support group out there?

Michael Josephson

Where There's a Will, There's a Way

According to the book *Nurture Assumption: Why Children Turn Out the Way They Do*, we grossly overestimate the power of parents to influence the kind of people their children become. Judith Rich Harris says that beyond their genetic contribution to temperament and predisposition, parents have virtually no impact.

Don't you believe it! Ms. Harris's conclusion is contrary to other research, and it contradicts common sense and human experience. So many of my behavior-motivating values came from my parents, it's hard to take her seriously. For instance, the phrase, "Where there's a will, there's a way. Where there's not, there's an alibi." My father drilled that into me and I hated it. It was always in the context of something I said I couldn't do. It drove me up the wall.

Yet I credit many of my successes to that drumbeat mantra he instilled in my head, and the example of him believing it. I can think of dozens of situations where this saying forced me to redouble my efforts rather than retreat.

Sure there are limits to the impact of parents. The formation of the enduring habits and beliefs that make up our character is an enormously complex process interweaving inborn personality traits with overt teaching, unconscious modeling and individual intellectual reactions to experiences. Yet it's a terrible mistake to undervalue the potential parents — and for that matter, teachers — have to shape the way a person processes information, deals with emotions and copes with stress and success.

No, parents alone cannot determine the character of their children, and some kids seem to resist any efforts to shape their values. But if you want to have a positive impact on your children's character, remember: "Where there's a will there's a way. Where there's not, there's an alibi." And the effort is profoundly important.

Five Things I Want My Kids to Know

Kids today! I've been struck by the inter-generational ritual where adults wring their hands in frustration over the unwillingness of kids to appreciate and accept their lessons of experience while youngsters stay confidently aloof, certain that the experiences and insights of their elders are simply too outdated to be taken seriously. Still, it's our job to try to pass on to the next generation as much wisdom as they're willing to take. There are five things I want my kids to know:

First, an essential step toward a truly happy life is to realize that selfishness and self-indulgence is ultimately self-defeating. It prevents meaningful relationships by building walls that isolate people from each other. Selfishness places too much emphasis on short-lived sensations of pleasure and fun and too little on understanding what's essential to true happiness.

Second, self-conscious attempts to establish individuality by being different — tattoos, nose rings, blue hair — obscure the reality that our true and indisputable uniqueness and identity is our character. Personal integrity is more than just doing what we feel like doing — it's having decent values about things that matter and living up to them.

Third, responsibility is part of life and the sooner we accept our responsibilities, the sooner we begin to build durable feelings of self-worth, self-respect and pride.

Fourth, no one can be happy unless he or she learns how to accept and deal with the fact that disappointments and failures are an inevitable part of life. We must learn how to be content even when we don't get everything we want.

Fifth, the surest road to happiness is to create and sustain meaningful personal relationships, and the three most important things to good relationships are trust, respect and kindness.

Michael Josephson

In Praise
of Mothers

My wife Anne is an extraordinary woman. She's beautiful, smart, funny, a wonderful companion and a great friend. But the quality I admire most is that she's an outstanding and thoroughly dedicated mother. And it takes dedication in my household of four little girls. Probably 90 percent of her waking hours are devoted to some aspect of mothering. As some Los Angeles-area billboards say, parenting is "the hardest job you'll ever love."

Our girls adore their mother, but until they have their own kids I don't think there's any chance that they will ever properly appreciate all she is and all she does for them. Planning what they'll eat and wear, picking the enrichment classes she'll take them to, feeding them, bathing them, consoling them, disciplining them, setting up play dates, buying gifts for the endless parade of children's birthday parties and nonstop chauffeuring — it's exhausting and mind-numbing.

Sure there's a payoff. The love and admiration of our little girls generates enough positive energy to light a city. But no matter how much we love our children, it takes character to so completely subordinate one's own life to the incessant, all-consuming life of active motherhood.

I know we can spoil children with excessive praise, but I don't think we can ever over-appreciate a mother. So, with Mother's Day coming up, it's time to sing the praises of mothers. It's time to pamper them and salute them.

Way to go, mothers! Especially you, Anne. Our children are lucky to have you in their lives.

Michael Josephson

The Not-So-Useless Old Man

Martin was 90. After a stroke, he moved in with his granddaughter Sarah and her daughter Lisa.

At first, 14-year-old Lisa would try to talk to him but Martin was so ashamed at his inability to speak clearly that he would only respond with grunts and gestures. She wanted to teach him to type notes on a computer, but he wouldn't try.

One evening, Lisa came to his room. She said she wanted to say good-bye, that she was pregnant from a boy who didn't love her, was desperately miserable and that she intended to kill herself that evening. He tried to say NO! NO! But she just kissed him on the cheek and went to her room.

Martin went to the computer and struggled to type a note, letter by letter. When he finished he pushed over a TV in his room to attract Lisa's attention and he fell hard in the process. Lisa came running and called an ambulance. After it took Martin to the hospital she noticed something on the computer screen. There were lots of typos but this is what he wrote:

"I do not speak because I cannot talk, not because I cannot think or feel. I feel helpless and used up and ashamed to be so useless. I gave up living and now you are giving up too. But your life is not hopeless. Maybe I'm not useless. You are smart and tender and loving. Your face is pretty, but your soul is beautiful. You are a wonderful gift to the world. Do not waste it because you are impatient that you have not yet found someone to appreciate you. It will happen. You must live so you can love and if you love you will live." He died that night. Lisa didn't.

Perhaps You're Happy and Don't Know It

I have often found weekends exhausting. At one time, with four little girls then all under seven, my wife Anne and I spent most of the waking hours dividing the tasks of chauffeuring them to dance and piano lessons, kids' parties and Sunday school; running errands; dressing Barbies; breaking up squabbles; cleaning up spills; playing constant waiter, valet and maid; and reading to them at night. I love being with my kids but it's hard work. One Sunday, I was particularly drained and short-tempered. Anne commented that I didn't seem happy. Was I happy? Well, it depends on how you define happiness.

Dennis Prager in his book *Happiness Is Serious Business* says that happiness is not so much an affirmative state of pleasure or contentment as it is the absence of unhappiness. In other words, if we're not unhappy, we're happy. To avoid unhappiness we can't have unrealistic expectations about a life overflowing with pleasure, fun and excitement. He urges lower expectations and warns that trying to compare our happiness to that of others usually makes us unhappy. Finally, we ought to prepare ourselves for the discovery that getting what we want doesn't necessarily result in happiness.

I think happiness is a bit more than that. For me, happiness is an affirmative state of mind, sense of fulfillment and gratitude for life spiced with occasional bursts of joy — like when my daughters giggle, hug each other spontaneously or say they love me. It's the smile that comes to my face uncontrollably when I pause to think about any one of them. So, am I happy? You bet I am, and I wouldn't trade my life for anyone's. Perhaps you're happy too and you don't know it.

Why Aren't More People Happy?

Ask struggling adolescents why they get high on drugs or alcohol or seek sex without intimacy or commitment and they're likely to tell you they just want to be happy. Ask young professionals why they're so driven to make money and they'll talk about all the things they'd get if they were rich, things that will make them happy. Ask adults why they had affairs or left their families and you'll hear it again: "I just want to be happy." So why aren't more people happy?

One problem is unrealistic expectations. Some people think of happiness as an unbroken series of pleasurable emotions, they hope to feel good all the time. Others expect a much more intense or lasting feeling of joy when they achieve a desired goal. As a result, when getting what they want doesn't produce the feelings they expected they fall into the kind of despondency conveyed in the famous Peggy Lee song: "Is That All There Is?"

There's great danger in confusing a sustainable state of happiness with fleeting sensations of pleasure and fun. Those who make pleasure-seeking the focus of their lives soon find themselves needing new and different sources of pleasure. It's like a drug addict who needs continually higher doses to get high.

Happiness is a less intense but more durable feeling of well-being. It's not a continuous state. No one is happy all the time. Though we may experience extraordinary moments of joy or despair, happiness is a kind of emotional resting place of quiet satisfaction with one's life. The art of living a happy life is a balance between getting what you want and learning to want what you get.

Michael Josephson

The Four Sources of Happiness

Last time we talked about happiness I suggested that it's a mistake to have unrealistic fantasies about the nature of happiness or to believe that the pursuit of money, power or sex can produce much more than transitory feelings of pleasure. So what does it take to achieve the more durable state of happiness? Traditionally, there are four main sources of real happiness: loving relationships, enjoyable work, service to others, and faith.

Let's start with relationships. Are you spending enough time and energy nurturing this dimension of life? I suppose it's possible to love what you do so much that you don't need other people, but more often than not, those who fail to develop and sustain meaningful relationships — friends, family, life partners — regret their priorities when they find themselves alone. And it's not just success-obsessed executives that lament the lost opportunities of loving and being loved. Ministers, teachers, police officers and politicians — people who devote their lives to serving others — are especially apt to neglect the people who they need (and who need them) the most.

Is your work likely to make you happy? Of course, not everyone has the luxury of having a job they love. Unfortunately, these kinds of jobs don't often pay well and, after all, a job is how one makes a living. Still, many people put up with boring or unpleasant work situations because they place too much weight on what they earn and where they work and too little on what they do. If work is not emotionally rewarding you may want to consider trade-offs as an investment in happiness.

Helen Keller said, "True happiness is not attained through self-gratification, but through fidelity to a worthy purpose." Albert Schweitzer said, "One thing I know: the only ones among you who will be really happy are those who will have sought and found how to serve." These observations should remind us of the peace of mind and sense of value one can get from faith and from devoting oneself to a worthy cause.

Character and Sports

Champions do not become champions when they win the event, but in the hours, weeks, months and years they spend preparing for it.

T. Alan Armstrong

Get Off Your Keister

During the holidays, my wife gave me racquetball gear and a basketball. I got the message: "Move your keister and get some exercise!" Actually, it was very thoughtful. In addition to the obvious concern about my health and fitness, it was affectionate encouragement. She knows I loved playing until injuries and scheduling excuses disrupted my routine and I drifted into a sedentary life. But that was 15 years ago! To say I'm out of shape is a wild understatement. I groan bending down to tie my shoe and grunt getting up from the couch.

Not understanding my fragile male ego, she instructed me to "just go out there and have fun!" Oh, if it were that easy. Sports isn't just recreation. It's competition. It's not enough to work up a sweat. You've got to be good. Or, at least, don't embarrass yourself. You'd think at my stage in life, ego considerations regarding athleticism would have atrophied along with my muscle tone. But there's a lot of pride involved, and the idea of starting again seemed preposterous and intimidating.

Then, that internal nag I call my conscience went to work on me, reminding me of all my talk about mustering the self-discipline and moral courage to confront and overcome fears, apathy and laziness. Like so many things — including getting a new job and starting new relationships — the hardest part is getting started, overcoming excuses and just doing it.

So I went down to my local Y and got a racquetball court so I could practice. It felt strange; it hurt; but soon I stopped whining and worrying and started enjoying it. Another two weeks and I'll be ready for competition.

The Tao of Racquetball

lready my re-entry into racquetball has yielded unexpected dividends. I've found that pounding a little rubber ball against a wall in an enclosed room 40 feet long, 20 feet wide and 20 feet high can reveal profound truths about life. Well, at least they seem profound at the time.

For example, in the past I often hurt myself crashing into walls or pulling muscles in a wanton pursuit of every shot. Now, I'm much more deliberate about what balls I go for. Sure, this new strategy was induced by my considerable physical limitations, but that doesn't dilute the wisdom of realizing how important it is in life to choose one's battles. If you go "all out" on every single play regardless of the likelihood of success, you may not have the resources to make more sensible efforts.

Yet, as I began to develop a little more agility and skill, I realized that I was giving up too often and too easily. Some balls were "gettable" with a reasonable but aggressive effort. Being too conservative is as unwise as indiscriminate recklessness. Yes, you should pick your battles, but be careful that timidity, fear or laziness don't blur your vision as to what's possible. You can't succeed at anything unless you push yourself beyond perceived limitations. We can all do more than we think we can.

Finally, my natural tendency was to try to win points by hitting the ball as hard as I could. In fact, placement and timing are much more important than raw power. I scored more often when I was strategic and thought about the angles. So it is with most of life's challenges. Think ahead, have a plan, use tact. It's a lot easier to persuade than pulverize the opposition.

True
Competitors

This is the final installment of my racquetball trilogy. I started my gradual re-entry to the sport practicing in privacy so I could rehearse without subjecting myself to pity or disdain. But a fellow saw me and offered to play a match. He was in much better shape than me, but then everyone is, so I accepted. He beat me soundly, but I had to face an inescapable truth: I love competition. It makes me try harder and helps me play better. And it's just plain fun.

Competition has been given a bad name by those who adopt win-at-any-cost tactics, like the fellow who was hiking in the woods with a friend. When they saw a bear looking right at them he declared, "I'm gonna run for it." His friend said, "You can't outrun a bear," but the fellow replied, "I don't have to, I just have to outrun you."

Much of American life has become obsessed with socially unhealthy and personally demeaning conceptions of competition. Unrestrained by principles of honor or decency, competitors view each other as enemies to be hated, humiliated, and destroyed.

John Naber, the great Olympic swimmer, taught me that "competition" comes from the Latin word *competere*, which means, "to strive together." Thus, real competition is a cooperative activity where competitors strive together to get the best out of themselves. True competitors appreciate and respect their opponents because without them there is no competition. The joy and glory of victory is not found in defeating others but in personal performance and pride that on this day they were faster, stronger or smarter.

True competitors love to test and stretch their skills, so they want worthy opponents on their best day. With this sort of attitude, true competitors don't always win, but they never lose.

Michael Josephson

Run, Shaya, Run!

Speaking at a dinner for a school for learning-disabled children, a father revealed pain and anguish when he wondered aloud about God's purpose in creating children who lack normal mental and physical capabilities. Then, he told this story:

While walking past a park where some boys were playing baseball, his son Shaya asked if he could play. One of the boys who knew that Shaya was not much of an athlete consented. His team was losing by six runs in the eighth inning and he saw no harm. Unexpectedly, however, his team scored, and when it was Shaya's turn to bat, the bases were loaded with two outs in the ninth inning.

Though they were within striking distance of victory, Shaya was allowed to come to the plate. He held the bat awkwardly so the pitcher stepped closer and lobbed the ball softly. Shaya swung clumsily and missed. A teammate helped him hold the bat and together they swung at the next pitch hitting a slow ground ball. After fielding it, the pitcher deliberately threw the ball over the first baseman's head.

Everyone started yelling, "Shaya, run to first. Run to first." Never in his life had Shaya run to first. Quickly, a silent pact of caring was forged among the boys and the right fielder followed the pitcher's lead by throwing the ball over the third baseman's head. Everyone yelled, "Keep running!" The shortstop turned the wide-eyed Shaya in the direction of third base and shouted, "Run to third." Then the boys from both teams screamed, "Run home." Shaya stepped on home plate with a glorious look of triumph and the boys lifted the game's hero on their shoulders. "That day," the speaker said, "I witnessed 18 boys reach their level of God's perfection."

Michael Josephson

No Matter How Prevalent, Cheating Is Still Wrong

What's happening to our culture? Why are we so afraid to judge harshly people who cheat? Is it because there is a little bit of cheating in all of us?

The reactions to my and others' outrage at the 2001 Little League Championship cheating scandal include a disturbing number of apologists who say that cheating is the American way. After all, in using overage kids, Rolando Paulino, the mastermind of the scheme, was simply doing what colleges and high schools have done for years: build a winning team by hook or by crook.

Hundreds of top athletes are coming to this country just to play sports and the placement of foreign students on college and high school teams by agents is becoming commonplace. Meanwhile, high-profile college programs spend great sums to aggressively recruit ringers — athletes with dubious qualifications and no real interest in getting a degree.

The high school athletic scene is getting just as bad. Athletic empire-building by private schools, including many with prominent religious affiliations, has become so accepted, that few people even see the moral implications anymore. In addition, so many parents are finding ways to place elite athletes at particular public schools that rules against recruiting are meaningless. As a result, leagues are becoming grossly unbalanced and aspiring athletes who go to their local schools are displaced, losing any real chance to play on teams filled with all-stars from all over. I'm told that cheating to win is even prevalent in the Special Olympics where adults overstate the disabilities of athletes to get a competitive edge.

I accept this as a reality but not as a new norm. There is no victory without honor. Cheating is wrong, very wrong. And people who do it ought to stop making excuses.

Michael Josephson

Little League Cheats Don't Win the Day

Danny Almonte was the 14-year-old pitcher who tore his way through the 12-and-under Little League in 2001, winning all 17 games he played. This disgraceful episode of cheating was perpetrated by Danny's father, who forged a birth certificate, and Rolando Paulino, a man with a long history of cheating who founded a league he named after himself.

Little League president Stephen Keener put it plainly and accurately: "Clearly, adults have used Danny Almonte and his teammates in a most contemptible and despicable way. Their actions are reprehensible."

It added fuel to the fire to learn that Almonte and Paulino had done the same thing with Danny's older brother. The scary thing is that the scam almost worked. The team placed third in the World Series, losing only because Danny could not pitch every game, and Danny received the kind of fame that legends and very large signing bonuses are made of.

Diligent efforts of suspicious opponents to prove Danny was a ringer had consistently failed. Only the persistence of a *Sports Illustrated* reporter uncovered the truth. To those who minimize the two-year difference, keep in mind that by pretending to be a 12-year-old Danny could throw his 70-mile-per-hour fastball from a mound 40 feet away. If he played kids his own age it would have been 60 feet.

Paulino and the Almontes stole opportunity from every team they played, but to the credit of the Little League organization that has fought mightily to assure that fair play and sportsmanship prevail, and some really classy parents and kids from College Park, Pennsylvania, and Oceanside, California (teams that suffered elimination in the regional and national finals), the virus of cheating failed to destroy the gratitude and good memories of the boys who played it straight.

A Walk-On Coach Leads the Way

Richmond High School near Oakland, California, is in the midst of poverty and violence. Many of its students don't take education very seriously and hope is in short supply. But in 1999 the school had one thing going for it: its winning-est basketball team ever. They were 13-0 when Coach Ken Carter made national news by benching his entire squad, locking them out of the gym, and forfeiting the next two games to emphasize his demand that his players take their studies seriously.

But that's not all. In a city plagued by gangs, he makes players sign and live up to an agreement requiring them to stay off the streets and maintain a 2.3 grade point average — higher than the state's minimum 2.0 GPA for sports participation. What's more, Carter's students not only must attend classes, but must sit in the front row.

The great thing is it all works. According to a July 2001 article in the *Los Angeles Times*, all 15 academic slackers on the 1999 team are going to college. This story is all the more remarkable since Carter isn't a full-time coach or even a member of the Richmond faculty. He's a walk-on coach who runs a sports supply store and a barbershop for a living.

But when he's with his team, Coach Carter knows he is, first and foremost, a teacher. Explaining his stance for academics, he said, "On the streets and public basketball courts in Richmond and any other city in America, you see the broken dreams of former high school legends who got left behind by life. And I'm not going to let that happen to these boys."

Carter's definition of winning it seems to be getting a college education for his athletes. With this definition, maybe winning *is* everything.

Heroes: Examples of Character

You gain strength, courage and confidence by every experience in which you must look fear in the face. You must do the thing you think you cannot do.

Eleanor Roosevelt

A Tribute to Lincoln

OK, I'm an Abraham Lincoln groupie. He is by every measure my biggest hero. My daughter Abrielle was named after him and our dog is named Lincoln. By sheer good fortune, my son Justin was born on Lincoln's birthday. I often visit the Lincoln Memorial and stand in awe of his magnificent eloquence and his legacy of honor, courage, compassion, humility and humor.

Yet in his own time he was more often ridiculed than revered. He was unmercifully belittled in the papers that often called him unrefined, simple, a bumpkin. He was ungainly, to some downright ugly.

But what a man! Self-educated, self-made, he was a skillful lawyer and effective politician whose character made his name almost synonymous with integrity. He was an inspirational leader who really believed in democracy — a government of the people, by the people, for the people. Empathy and compassion were in his blood. He felt the pain of others as deeply as any man could, yet duty made him a leader of our nation's bloodiest war.

Now one of the most esteemed men in all history, Lincoln was often depressed by feelings of inadequacy. Groucho Marx once joked, "I wouldn't want to be in any club that would have me." But the original source for this classic line was none other than a young, self-effacing Abraham Lincoln who quite seriously wrote to a woman who rejected his marriage proposal: "I can never be satisfied with anyone who would be blockhead enough to have me." It's interesting, in a world that places such a high value on self-esteem, that one of America's truest and greatest heroes was genuinely, perhaps excessively, humble.

Dr. King: An Authentic Hero

The pages of history are full of stories about people I greatly admire, but I have three main heroes: Abraham Lincoln, Mahatma Gandhi and Martin Luther King, Jr. According to the dictionary, a hero is "a person noted for feats of courage or nobility of purpose, especially one who has risked or sacrificed his or her life."

I think each of these men fits this definition perfectly. It disturbs me, however, how often I run into people who undervalue Dr. King's contributions. Sometimes there's the snide inference that the Martin Luther King holiday is just another form of affirmative action. I find such cynicism baffling. Dr. King was not simply a great black man. He was, in every respect, a great American hero.

Read his speeches and weigh them in the context of his times. Study his actions and his ability to resist enormous pressures — from those who thought he was going too far and those who thought he wasn't going far enough — and it's evident that he was an extraordinary inspirational leader with uncommon vision and strength. He has as great a claim to the title of prophet as any man in the century.

But Dr. King didn't simply talk about his dreams; he went to the battle lines time and time again to fight for them. He devoted his too-short life to bringing us closer to a more compassionate and just world where, in his words, people would be judged, not by the color of their skin, but the content of their character. He was murdered before he reached the age of 40 in the midst of that fight.

I'm impatient with those who would disqualify him from hero status for his personal flaws — allegations of infidelity and plagiarism. A person doesn't have to be perfect to be a hero. It's quite enough that he makes a better world.

Michael Josephson

Coach Wooden, the Philosopher

According to Henry David Thoreau, a philosopher is a person who seeks to understand and solve the most serious problems of life, not only theoretically, but practically. A true philosopher, Thoreau added, is so committed to wisdom that he seeks to live wisely and therefore lives a life of simplicity, independence, magnanimity and trust. By this definition, John Wooden, my favorite coach and teacher, is every inch a great American philosopher. Here are just a few of his powerful insights.

On Perfection: "Perfection is an impossibility, but striving for perfection is not. Do the best you can. That is what counts."

On Management: "You'll get better cooperation and results if you are sincerely interested in people's families and interests, not simply how they do their job."

On Learning: "Learn as if you were going to live forever, and live as if you were going to die tomorrow."

On Success: "You must be interested in finding the best way, not in having your own way."

On Trust: "You will be hurt occasionally if you trust too much, but you will live in torment if you do not trust enough."

On Joy: "Mix idealism with realism and add hard work. This will often bring much more than you could ever hope for."

On Winning: "If you prepare properly, you may be outscored but you will never lose. You always win when you make the full effort to do the best of which you're capable."

You can read more in the Coach's newest book, *Be Quick — But Don't Hurry* with Andrew Hill, and in *Wooden: A Lifetime of Observations and Reflections On and Off the Court* with Steve Jamison.

Coach Wooden's Favorite Mementos

When I first visited Coach John Wooden's home I was struck by how much it is like the coach himself — an understated, unpretentious condominium that he was totally comfortable in. Still, I thought, it was too small for such a great man. It was cluttered with pictures of his children, grandchildren and great-grandchildren. Books and countless large and small plaques, awards and inscribed gifts filled almost every inch of tabletop, wall and bookshelf space.

The stuff was not displayed as a matter of "look what I got" pride but rather as a sign of respect for the person who gave it to him. It's not his nature to dishonor or trivialize any gesture of appreciation.

I asked him whether any of the mementos had special meaning. He said he especially treasures recognition for things other than the success of his basketball teams, which, he says, was earned by the talent of his players. He showed me a Big Ten medal he won in 1932 for athletics and scholarship, a medal he was awarded for humanitarianism, and a picture of one of his heroes, Mother Teresa. And then he read me this poem written to him by Sven Nader, a former player:

I saw love once./ I saw it clear./ It had no leash./ It had no fear.
It gave itself/ Without a thought./ No reservation/ Had it bought.
It seemed so free/ To demonstrate./ It seemed obsessed / To orchestrate
A symphony./ Designed to feed, / Composed to lift,/ The one in need.
Concern for others/ Was its goal,/ No matter what/ Would be the toll.
It's strange just how/ Much care it stores/ To recognize/ Its neighbor's sores
And doesn't rest/ Until the day/ It's helped to take/ The sores away.
Its joy retains/ And does not run/ Until the blessing's/ Job is done.
I saw love once./ 'Twas not pretend./ He was my coach./ He is my friend.

A Doctor Who Cares

Dr. Fred Epstein specializes in children with brain tumors. He's one of the best in the world, but, as good as he is, he regularly has to deal with youngsters he can't save. And when these patients die he must deal with parents whose grief and pain can shatter souls. So it wouldn't be surprising if the good doctor retreated behind a wall of professional objectivity to shield himself from the emotions of death and dying.

But he doesn't. Instead, he makes a special effort to be sure that he and his associates never lose sight of the humanity of his patients. According to an article in *Modern Maturity*, while Dr. Epstein was addressing a conference, he unfolded a piece of paper. It was a poem from a teenage boy found by his parents after he died.

Why do I live?
I have prayed in the night
By the cold and lonely side of my bed
And I still wonder: Will I be saved?
I ask you reader, whoever you may be,
Take my trembling hand and warm it with care
and sympathy.

"I always felt I failed this boy," he said. "I kept thinking of his line about sitting alone in a cold room and there's no one to hold his hand. And I thought: We doctors have been arrogant. We've been so focused on technology that we haven't paid attention to what the living person is going through."

So when he had the chance to start an Institute for Neurology at a prominent New York hospital, he dedicated himself to creating an environment pervaded with genuine caring and love.

"Please don't let me die," a boy pleaded before a surgery. When he began the operation he announced to his colleagues, "This is a 10-year-old boy from a small Southern town. His parents love him a lot. He's an only child, and he plays soccer. Let's make sure he'll play soccer again."

Michael Josephson

Character and Society

He that would make his own liberty secure must guard even his enemy from oppression; for if he violates this duty he establishes a precedent that will reach to himself.

Thomas Paine

Self-Esteem: The Good, the Bad and the Ugly

If you've ever seen a child or had a friend who truly suffers through life because of the fears and insecurities caused by low self-image you know why so many educators and psychologists stress the importance of self-esteem. And it's not just a matter of feeling good. Substantial evidence supports the idea that deep emotional and social problems can be traced to low expectations, a sense of hopelessness, even self-hate generated by a lack of self-esteem. It can produce fatalistic ("what difference does it make?") young people who hurt themselves or others. In the next few commentaries I want to talk about the good, the bad and the ugly of the modern-day self-esteem movement. Let's start with the good.

Concern with self-esteem blossomed into a full-blown movement in the 1980s as an army of sociologists, psychologists and educators began to present theories and evidence that low self-esteem — a limiting self-image based on feelings of inadequacy — was one of the greatest barriers to achievement for a large portion of the population.

They properly took to task parents and teachers who ignore principles of respect and kindness and do great psychic damage by delivering confidence-shattering assessments that someone is worthless, won't ever amount to anything or is just plain bad. Such accusations can program the victims of verbal abuse to fulfill negative expectations. Studies show that low self-esteem is linked to crime, violence, alcohol and drug abuse, teen pregnancy, child abuse, welfare dependency and poor academic performance. Many say it is a "primary causal factor." What's more, self-destructive and antisocial behavior can be significantly reduced if kids can be taught to reject negative self-assessments in favor of self-respect and confidence. And from an ethical perspective, it's cruel, disrespectful and misleading to belittle or minimize a child's sense of the possible.

The Bad and the Ugly: Self-Esteemia

Sometimes a good idea generates zealots who take the idea too far. There is a good side of the self-esteem movement, as I have said. But here I want to take a look at the bad and the ugly. I call it "self-esteemia," the toxic effect of worrying too much about *feeling* good and too little about *being* good.

The roots of the self-esteem movement can be found in therapeutic models of mental health concerned with personal happiness and self-actualization. Its focus is not on character but contentment. That would be fine if it weren't for the negative side effects.

What has happened is that too often ardent builders of self-esteem have become so preoccupied with making people feel good about themselves that they have ignored issues of ethics and character. But unless self-esteem is associated with being a good person and living a moral life, it can turn out to be no more than a form of amoral narcissism. And since much of the literature of the self-esteem movement tends to redefine selfishness in a positive way and advocate freeing oneself from the moral burdens of shame and guilt, self-esteemia can actually disable the conscience.

To foster self-esteem, parents and teachers are told that all verbal and nonverbal messages should be positive and affirming, consistent with the mantra "you are responsible, able and valuable." Many self-esteemists seem to think that a child's self-image is so fragile that it can't withstand the slightest negative input. Even saying no is to be avoided. As a result, parents and teachers are told to withhold even honest and constructive moral criticisms thereby denying youngsters standards of moral judgment. Thus self-esteemia soon manifests itself in mindless non-judgmentalness, a world where there is no right and wrong.

Healthy Self-Esteem Is Built on Character

As the last part of my self-esteem trio, I'd like to explore how we eliminate the bad and ugly aspects of self-esteemia while keeping the important effects of promoting strong self-respect.

Let's start with the principle that all people, including kids of every age and condition, are intrinsically worthy, and they should be taught that at an early age. I heard a story of a little girl who was called "worthless" and "hopeless" by a classmate. The girl responded confidently that this just wasn't so.

"How can you be so sure?" asked her friend.

"Cause God made me, and God don't make no garbage."

Of course, we should instill in youngsters self-respect and self-confidence, teaching them, by words and actions, that they have limitless potential — to learn, to overcome setbacks, to be happy and to be people of admirable character. Our goal is not simply to make children feel good about themselves but to make them feel good about being good.

We should avoid indiscriminate approval that blinds children to their faults. We should mix sincere praise and encouragement with kind but honest feedback that reinforces clear boundaries of right and wrong. Whatever we do to instill a strong conscience is a gift. We should teach children that their power to make choices in attitudes, effort and conduct creates responsibility and that feelings of shame and guilt are a natural consequence of irresponsible choices.

Gary Trudeau offers this insight at the conclusion of a Doonesbury comic strip: "Isn't it possible that self-esteem isn't causal at all, but simply the happy side effect of a sturdy character, itself the product of unambiguous moral education?"

Michael Josephson

My Friend Julie

I'm not proud to admit that kindness is not always my first instinct. I'm struggling to get better, but my unreflective reactions are more likely to be critical than complimentary. And I often don't take the time to get off my task-driven freight train to follow through on the good impulses I do have to offer a helping hand or even write a thoughtful note.

That's why I'm so glad to have a friend like Julie, a very busy mother of two young children who seems to have an endless instinct and capacity to help others. No matter how hectic her own life is, she's the first to offer a hand to watch someone else's kids, make and deliver meals, or drive here or there to rescue a friend. Her generosity is inspiring whether she is helping an elderly neighbor shop or adopting a family every

Christmas. She even sends me e-mails full of nice stories I can use for commentaries.

When I'm not sure what the kind thing to do is, all I have to do is ask: "What would Julie do?" That's what a real role model is. Not some remote celebrity but a person in our lives who shows us by her actions how we should be.

The English novelist George Eliot said: "The presence of a noble nature, generous in its wishes, ardent in its charity, changes the lights for us." Such a person leads us to believe that we too can be better, kinder, more giving and helpful. Longfellow talked about how great men leave their footprints on the sands of time. Well, there are also great people who leave their fingerprints on our hearts. Our friend Julie is one of those.

Michael Josephson

What I've Learned (1)

I want to share with you an edited version of a poem I came across on the Internet. I don't know the true source, but it's chock-full of wisdom.

I've learned — that no matter how much I care, some people just don't care back.

I've learned — that it's not what you have in your life but who you have in your life that counts.

I've learned — that you can get by on charm for about 15 minutes. After that, you'd better know something.

I've learned — that it's taking me a long time to become the person I want to be.

I've learned — that it's a lot easier to react than it is to think.

I've learned — that you can keep going long after you think you can't.

I've learned — that we are responsible for what we do, no matter how we feel.

I've learned — that either you control your attitude or it controls you.

I've learned — that money is a lousy way of keeping score.

I've learned — that no matter how good a friend is, they're going to hurt you every once in a while and you must forgive them for that.

I've learned — that it isn't always enough to be forgiven by others. Sometimes you have to learn to forgive yourself.

I've learned — that no matter how badly your heart is broken, the world doesn't stop for your grief.

I've learned — that two people can look at the exact same thing and see something totally different.

I've learned — that the people you care most about in life are taken from you too soon.

I've learned — that it's hard to determine where to draw the line between being nice and not hurting people's feelings, and standing up for what you believe.

Michael Josephson

What I've Learned (2)

I am inspired to write my own version of the anonymous Internet poem called "What I've Learned."

I've learned — that I'm a work in progress. And that there will always be a gap between who I am and who I want to be.

I've learned — that I don't have to be sick to get better. And that every single day brings opportunities to improve my character.

I've learned — that it's easier to talk about integrity than to live it. And that the true test is my willingness to do the right thing even when it costs more than I want to pay.

I've learned — that I judge myself by my best intentions but that I am judged by my worst acts.

I've learned — that terrible things will happen but that I can overcome any tragedy.

I've learned — that pain is inevitable but suffering is optional. And that I have as much control over my attitudes as my actions.

I've learned — that winning really isn't everything. And that there is no real victory without honor.

I've learned — that when I fight fire with fire, all I get is the ashes of my own integrity.

I've learned — that kind words really matter, but that it takes a conscientious effort to be kind. And that thoughtless comments and badly timed criticisms can cause serious hurt.

I've learned — that it can take years to build up trust and only seconds to destroy it.

I've learned — that I have to remind myself to be grateful for all I have. And that forgiving is much harder to do than to say.

I've learned — that happiness is much deeper and enduring than pleasure. And that I am solely responsible for my own happiness.

I've learned — that no one is happy all the time, but that I can be as happy as I'm willing to be.

I've learned — that the surest road to happiness is good relationships. And that to have good relationships, I've got to be a good person.

Michael Josephson

Workplace Ethics

*A person of character
takes as much trouble
to discover what is right
as lesser men take to
discover what will pay.*

Confucius

The Camera I Didn't Buy

I needed a new camera. And if I didn't have it before my wife went into labor I would never forgive myself — and that would be the least of my grief. Since I hate to shop, I'm a big mail order fan. So I bought a photography magazine, picked a camera and comparison shopped by studying the ads in the back. The rest was supposed to be easy. It wasn't.

I called the 800 number and told the man what I wanted. First, he tried to switch me to a more expensive lens. I was tempted, but I resisted. I wasn't even sure it was a better lens. Already, I didn't trust him.

"How about an ultraviolet lens filter?"
"No thanks. What's my total?"

"Well, I can give you the better lens in a special package with the warranty for . . ." After a lot of fast-talking mumbo jumbo, he finally gave me my total plus $35 for shipping and handling.

"For a little camera?"

"That's our price — nobody will do it for less — but I'll give you five dollars off on the filter."

"I didn't order a filter."

"But you should, and you should get our extended warranty, only $10 a year."

"How long is it?"

"Seven years."

"So it's $70?"

"I guess you could say that."

I got testy at this point so he got offended. "Hey, I'm on your side." I didn't think so and hung up. I still need a new camera.

I know aggressive sales tactics of this sort are common, but the bottom line is I distrusted the salesman, resented his fast-talking cons and little deceptions and felt disrespected. And I'm going to send a copy of this commentary to the owner of the company so he'll know.

Michael Josephson

How Much
Is Two
Plus Two?

selection committee of the board of
directors was assigned the task of hiring a new CEO. The chairman decided
to ask only one question: "How much is two
plus two?"

The first candidate was the chief financial
officer. Baffled by the question, he answered
straightforwardly, "It's four."

The second candidate was a chief engineer
from the company's research lab. He proudly
answered that the result depends on whether the
twos were positive twos or negative twos. The
answer could be minus four, zero or plus four.

The sales manager was more creative: "Well,
the way I look at it, two plus two is 22."

Finally, they brought in legal counsel. He wrote the question down on a yellow legal pad, looked directly in the eyes of the questioner and said: "How much do you want it to be?"

This story illustrates how easy and tempting it is to suspend any notion that we should be candid and truthful in answering questions. And it's not just lawyers and politicians who succumb to the temptation. Lots of us delude ourselves into thinking it's part of the game to give an answer we think the interviewer wants to hear. So we lie to potential employers, government bureaucrats and others as if it is our right to do so.

This is not only dishonest, but in many cases it's counterproductive. Experienced interviewers can usually tell when they are being conned. And it doesn't make a good impression.

I'm sure some companies place a higher value on cleverness than credibility, but anyone worth working for wants integrity. It's often hard to be honest when we think the truth will be used to our disadvantage, but to a person of character there's no choice.

It Never Occurred to Me That I Was a Failure

I t was six months since Mac graduated from college and he wasn't making much progress finding a job. "I want a job I can enjoy," he told his father, who managed a muffler shop. His dad responded, "Son, they call it 'work' for a reason. Get a job to make a living so you can get on with your life." Mac shot back, "I don't want to waste my life managing a muffler shop. I've got higher standards."

Obviously hurt, his father said, "Don't you think I wished for an easier or more prestigious or better paying job? But you know what? I've had to face up to the fact that I didn't have the talent to play pro hockey or be a sportswriter. And I'm no business genius. But don't tell me I wasted my life. I've given you and your two sisters a good home and college educations, I love your mother and I'm respected in the community. Until now, it never occurred to me that I might be a failure." And he left the room.

Mac's mother was furious. "We don't begrudge you your ambitions but how dare you demean another man's life? Here's our definition of success." She handed him a folded newspaper clipping of an old Ann Landers column with a poem by Betty Anderson Stanley:

"He has achieved success who has lived well, laughed often and loved much; who has enjoyed the trust of pure women, the respect of intelligent men and the love of little children; who has filled his niche and accomplished his task; who has left the world better than he found it, whether by an improved poppy, a perfect poem, or a rescued soul; who has never lacked appreciation of Earth's beauty or failed to express it; who has always looked for the best in others and given them the best he had; whose life was an inspiration; whose memory a benediction."

Filling Holes: The Responsibilities of Employees

You may have heard the story about two fellows hard at work alongside a road. One diligently dug holes while the other waited a short interval and then filled them up.

It all seemed rather foolish and eventually the workers were confronted by a supervisor who demanded an explanation. The fellow who dug the holes asked what the problem was. He said he had been doing the same job for more than 10 years. His cohort quickly chimed in that he had been filling the holes for the same period.

Upon further questioning, they admitted it made more sense in the past when a third fellow worked with them. His job had been to put a new tree into the hole. But when he retired he was never replaced so the two just kept on working as before.

"Why didn't you tell somebody?" the supervisor sputtered. "My gosh, you signed Phil's retirement letter. We figured you knew."

The kinds of unproductive, inefficient and even counterproductive practices that go on in most workplaces defy logic and reveal a great deal about character. You see, the ethical principle of responsibility includes a moral duty to make things better, to pursue excellence and to produce and demand quality. Yet basically good people in virtually every workplace regularly engage in or witness some process or practice that is unhelpful, wasteful or even harmful to the ultimate goals of the organization.

While management is ultimately to blame, people of character shouldn't passively demean the value of their work by becoming part of anything second-rate or stupid. It may take tact and timing, maybe even some courage, but it's our duty to be a force for excellence. The benefit is that the quality of our lives improves dramatically when we take pride in our work.

Responsibilities of Being Boss

As I speak to business groups around the country, I frequently hear senior executives utter modern clichés about wanting employees to "think outside the box," to take risks, to be creative. And while I'm sure companies truly appreciate breakthrough ideas that increase profits, productivity or quality, the problem is that the culture in most organizations is quite inhospitable to those who challenge old ways of doing things, including practices that make no sense or are simply inefficient.

An often overlooked obligation of ethical management is to establish an atmosphere where employees are truly expected and willing to accept responsibility for improving the quality of programs, products and procedures — even if it means challenging well-established policies or management decisions. Though most managers think they're open to ideas, Josephson Institute studies show that one-third of employees say there's a "kill the messenger" tradition where they work that discourages suggestions and promotes concealment of negative information. Whenever a manager asks, "Why didn't someone tell me?" it's time to find ways to more effectively send the message that mission-oriented employees who produce and demand quality are to be prized, not penalized.

I think every manager has the ultimate responsibility to assure that practices and procedures are efficient, effective and consistent with organizational values and goals. This requires a full, hands-on, detailed knowledge of what subordinates actually do and an understanding of how things really work.

Michael Josephson

The Centipede and Job References

A centipede with sore legs hired a consultant. After studying the situation, the consultant came up with a solution: "When your legs start to hurt, just fly in the air for a few minutes to take the weight off." The centipede loved the idea but he asked, "Since I don't have wings, how can I get into the air?" The consultant was disdainful. "That's implementation. I just do policy."

Perhaps my advice about hiring for character and training for skills is equally impractical. While theoretically an employer could make an intelligent decision about the character of a prospective employee based on comprehensive and candid references from former employers, myths about the law and fear of litigation have virtually shut off this valuable source of information.

Many human resources professionals are under the false impression that they cannot give complete and honest references. This is the result of a self-protective lawyer strategy to limit even the possibility of defamation litigation by instructing employers not to disclose even well-documented information about former employees.

As a result, companies and public agencies regularly play "pass the meatball" by giving former employees with serious character flaws virtual immunity. The funny thing is that in many states, including California, there is a strong public policy in favor of honest and complete job references. Special laws have been passed that require former employees not only to prove that reference information was false and defamatory, but also to prove that it was conveyed maliciously or without good faith. In fact, a recent California Supreme Court case held an employer liable for failing to convey relevant information about the sexual misconduct of a former employee.

Of course, employers should be scrupulously fair and accurate in giving negative employee references, but I think there's a moral obligation to reveal relevant information, especially where serious physical or economic harm could result.

Michael Josephson

Getting the References You Want

Let's talk about ways an employer committed to hiring people of character can get better information.

First, you can require job applicants to sign a waiver explicitly authorizing former employers to honestly and fully disclose information concerning job performance and character. Though such waivers are technically not required (freedom of speech always protects employers who give honest and accurate information), they may convince timid employers to be more forthcoming. Such waivers are common in law enforcement and other character-sensitive positions and they can be worded so they even nullify written nondisclosure agreements. To be fair, the prospective employer should give the applicant an opportunity to discuss and explain any negative information.

Second, an explanation of the importance you attach to character followed by direct and focused questions can often result in fuller disclosure. It can also create liability if the former employer does not disclose relevant information. Here are some sample questions:

1. The job we are considering the applicant for requires a high degree of personal integrity and ethics. Do you have any information that bears on this issue?
2. We have special concerns about issues of safety. Do you have any information that might indicate the employee has a propensity toward violence or unsafe conduct?
3. I've described the job we are interviewing for. Is there any information you have that you would want to know if you were in my position?
4. Regardless of how the termination was actually characterized, was the employee fired or asked to resign?

Crisis and Character

No passion so effectually robs the mind of all its powers of acting and reasoning as fear.

Edmund Burke

What We Should Remember

hen I experienced the assassination of President John F. Kennedy, I learned about mortality and the power of evil. No one I knew would have believed that a single fanatic with a rifle could kill the president of the United States. Not in 1963. Then, in 1968, the murders of Martin Luther King, Jr. and Robert Kennedy brought a final end to the innocence of my generation.

On September 11, 2001, the world witnessed how far we've come as zealots armed with box-cutters committed murder of unimaginable proportions. Driven by hatred for America, they killed nearly 5,000 people of many nationalities. In a few hours, exclamation points were added to the insight that human life is fragile and that no person, no monument, no civilization is safe from the forces of evil. So what should we remember?

We should remember that every single life is precious and that it is right and necessary that we grieve and suffer on behalf of every single father, mother, husband, wife, brother, sister and friend whose crushed and disintegrated remains are buried within the rubble of the World Trade Center.

We should remember that our ability to cry for strangers proves we are not like the coldhearted bigots who caused this calamity and that we should not callously kill innocents to get revenge.

We should remember that anger is only one letter short of danger and that we must not allow ourselves or our nation to succumb to the kind of blind rage and consuming hatred that dehumanized the terrorists who brutalized our society.

We should remember that our sense of civility and humanity is not universal and that hatred and prejudice produce a deadly virus. Though our enemies regard Americans as an indistinguishable group of humans unworthy of compassion or respect, we must guard against similar prejudices against Arabs, Muslims or Middle Easterners.

Michael Josephson

What Will Terrorism Do to Us?

I t may take a while to discover the impact that the terrorist attacks in New York and Washington will have on our personal and national character. One thing is for sure: the calamity of September 11, 2001, will have a lasting impact on the American psyche. Terrorism isn't new, but it's never occurred on this scale before, and we can't escape the implications of this conclusive evidence of our vulnerability to instantaneous mass destruction.

In the days following this attack we saw close-ups of horrible carnage, and we will continue to be confronted with choices that could change us as individuals and alter the nature of our society. Filled with compassion, fear, rage and a desire for revenge, we can emerge more caring or more callous.

We know that mortality statistics can't begin to convey the personal grief behind those numbers. And while compassion and empathy are important qualities of character, they can cause pain. It's tempting to shield ourselves by turning away, but if we do, we risk becoming desensitized and we lose the opportunity to fortify our instinct to care. We should realize that embedded within the headlines are tens of thousands of individual tragedies, and we must force ourselves to stay emotionally engaged because it strengthens our humanity.

It can be sad and depressing, but if we allow ourselves to imagine with our hearts what is being felt by every single child who became an orphan, every parent who lost a child, or each husband and wife suddenly divorced by death, we are more likely to help others — and to become better people.

The Day My Rabbi Cried

On the heels of the September 11th terrorist killings, Rabbi Stephen Carr Reuben's large congregation in Los Angeles was anxious to hear their charismatic leader's Rosh Hashanah sermon. He hoped to inspire his audience with stories of love and valor and invocations about faith and courage, and he started strong, but after a few minutes his confident, soothing voice broke, and all could see the enormity of the evil and the intensity of the pain overtake him. He stopped and put away his prepared text.

With tears welling in his eyes, he told of the call he received from his daughter from a phone booth near the World Trade Center. She was a horrified and hysterical witness to unimaginable death and destruction. As a father and a rabbi he consoled her by giving her perspective, support, and just by being there.

Soon after, he saw the dreadful images himself, and, like the rest of us, he felt soul-wrenching outrage, grief and pity. But he had a job to do: to be a source of wisdom and strength. So he held it together as he counseled and encouraged frightened, confused and suffering congregants.

But in the midst of his prepared sermon, he realized this was not a time to hold back tears, but a time to cry, and that what he and others needed most wasn't inspiration but comfort — not with parables and profound insights, but with loving touches. It was a time to hold and be held. And so this brave and deeply good man cried and told of his need to be comforted.

He gave us permission to grieve, and we cried — for him, for all the victims and for the world — and we learned how lonely it can be to be strong, and that even comforters need to be comforted.

Michael Josephson

Defenses More Dangerous Than Our Enemies

The terrorist attacks in New York and Washington are a challenge to our national character.

Terrorism has never occurred on this scale. The attack on the Marine barracks in Beirut killed 241; 270 people died from the downing of Pan Am flight 103; 169 were killed in Oklahoma City; six in the first World Trade Center attack; and 17 in the terrorist attack on the USS Cole. At Pearl Harbor, about 2,400 were killed. The death toll on the morning of September 11 greatly exceeded all these tragedies combined.

As a frantic desire to lay blame and find solutions envelops public discourse, some of the distinguishing characteristics of American policy will be challenged. We have to be careful not to compromise principles that have defined our national character.

I'm not worried about overreaction against the perpetrators of this mass murder (if they can be identified with reasonable certainty). Both my sense of justice and belief in the value of deterrence justifies a swift and strong reaction.

I am worried that our hunger for retribution can lead us to adopt policies that overcome our best instincts and values. In the aftermath of Pearl Harbor, we turned our backs on our most cherished traditions and created internment camps, literally imprisoning thousands of innocent and loyal Americans of Japanese descent.

Ethnic stereotyping and talk about mass retaliation, removing prohibitions on assassinations, and giving the FBI and CIA expanded powers challenge our sense of propriety and civility. Anger and fear are natural but if we are not thoughtful, our defenses could be more dangerous than our enemies.

Michael Josephson

Forsake Revenge, But Pursue Justice and Self-Defense

I admit it: though I still suffer surges of sadness, compassion and grief for the victims, I think more and more about making the monsters who killed and maimed all those people on September 11, 2001, pay for their crime. I want our country to hunt down every planner, facilitator and conspirator of that hideous event. I want justice. And I want revenge. But revenge and justice are two separate concepts.

The instinct for retribution, the desire to inflict pain on those who cause us pain, may be primitive but it's part of human nature. It's certainly part of my nature. Yet I realize it's not the best part. Revenge is fueled by rage and hate, qualities that need to be constrained, not encouraged. Yes, it's human to want revenge, but the lust for vengeance can desensitize us in ways that lead to cruel and callous behavior that demeans us as individuals and as a nation. It's one thing to be human; it's another to be humane.

I support our national resolve to ferret out and punish everyone guilty of this horrendous murder, and our willingness to take dramatic steps to prevent future attacks. But we can do what needs to be done without resorting to unhealthy and dangerous vengeful motives and tactics.

We can justify the relentless pursuit of those who knowingly facilitated this crime on the independent grounds of self-defense and justice. Dedicated terrorists present a clear and present danger, and it is both moral and prudent that we protect ourselves. In addition, principles of justice require that criminals be held accountable for their crimes and that they suffer consequences that fit their crimes.

Whatever the motive, we may end up in the same place, but in issues of morality motives mean a lot. I just hope we take the high road.

Our Moral Obligation to Overcome Fear

Our economy is in deep trouble. Tens of thousands of men and women, most with families that depend on them, have lost their jobs and many more will if we don't pull ourselves together and get back to living normal, healthy lives. I know in the wake of the September 11th attacks that we will never be the same, but we can't let a tiny band of ruthless fanatics dismantle our way of living.

The most powerful cause of our economic woes is fear. The way to get ourselves out of the tailspin is by mustering the moral courage to face and overcome fear.

Individuals who let their fears control them subject themselves to the throbbing torture of continuous anxiety. They allow happy thoughts,

---

pleasurable feelings and hopeful dreams to be strangled by a growing vine of angst, and they imprison themselves with worries that prevent them from traveling, assembling with others in large crowds or spending money.

But as I've seen traveling through airports these individual fears have a dramatic impact on others. They are crippling our economy, which needs people to travel, assemble and spend. Each of us has a moral obligation to escape from fear for our own sake and for the sake of our fellow citizens. It's a moral obligation that challenges and tests our character.

Yes, fear comes uninvited as part of the aftershock of tragedy. But it can't stay and live with us unless we feed it. I'm going to talk more in the next two commentaries about what we can do, but for now here are the main strategies: eliminate fear by being realistic about the risks, and overcome the fears you can't eliminate by courageous acts of will.

Michael Josephson

Three Reasons Not to Be Afraid

Fear is the wayward son of Prudence and Wisdom. In moderation, it can be a good thing, warning us of dangers and inducing us to resist urges to be rash or reckless. The problem is that Fear has no perspective and it doesn't know when to stop. As a result, Fear and its children, Anxiety, Worry and Dread, can grip us so tightly that they strangle our ability to get pleasure from our lives.

So it is with the individuals and companies who refuse to fly or buy and the people purchasing gas masks and antibiotics for anthrax. Though safety concerns are not groundless, the new security measures probably make airline travel safer than ever, and the risks of chemical or germ warfare are very small. Here are three good reasons to refuse to be afraid:

First, it's irrational. This is such a huge country, with literally thousands of potential targets, that the likelihood of any individual being victimized is akin to the chance of winning the lottery.

Second, such fear is useless. In the 1950s, the nation was so obsessed with an overblown fear of the atom bomb that every child was terrorized by "drop drills." The idea was that any teacher who spotted a nuclear bomb mushroom out the window would yell "Drop!" so all children could curl under their desks. Aside from the unreality of the premise, the action would have been of no value had a bombing occurred.

Third, fear is endless. The world is full of everyday dangers far more likely than terrorism: drunk and reckless drivers, domestic criminals, heart attacks and stroke, and even food poisoning. Before we give up air travel we should give up driving and stay locked in our homes. And if we're going to be afraid, let's worry about alienated teenagers with rifles, road rage, nuclear power accidents, earthquakes, fires and floods.

Four Reasons to Master Fear

Irrational fearfulness causes us to exaggerate risks and leads to endless and useless anxiety. Yet I know not everyone can eliminate fears through logic. That's why we need to muster the will to proceed despite our fears. Mark Twain was right: courage is not the absence of fear but mastery of it. Here are four reasons to master our fears:

First: Fear is a form of continuous suffering. When we let worry, anxiety and dread control our lives we pay continuous tribute to fear through self-inflicted torment. It's like paying blackmail to an extortionist. Thus, we suffer whether or not the event we fear ever comes about. That's why they say a coward dies a thousand deaths.

Second: Fearfulness is a bad example for our kids. Nothing scares children more than frightened parents. If we want confident and courageous children we have to show them that we too have fears but that we will not be owned by them.

Third: We get stronger every time we defeat fear. As Eleanor Roosevelt said, every time we confront our fears without surrender we get stronger. Every time we live through a horror, do what we thought we could not do, we gain the courage and confidence we need to deal with whatever comes along.

Fourth: Changing our lives out of fear rewards terrorists and encourages further attacks. Just as paying off hijackers generates more hijackings, acting terrified spawns more terrorism. Strength of character in the face of threats and attacks is as important to our national defense as is military strength. We defeat terrorism by refusing to be terrified.

Didi's Ordeal and Triumph

Blessed with unusual beauty, intelligence and talent, Didi embraced life with both hands and gulped it down boldly. Shielded by a youthful sense of invulnerability she traveled all over the world as a singer meeting everyone she could and making friends of everyone she met. Didi was bold and fearless — until the night a man broke into her apartment, woke her from a peaceful sleep, and raped her at knifepoint. The rapist not only violated her body, but ravaged her mind, infecting it with the virus of fear that produces chronic dread and episodic feelings of outright terror.

She no longer looked at life through the window of naïve innocence. She would never again enter her car or apartment at night without heart-pounding apprehension, and she often has to summon up courage just to be alone.

That was 25 years ago, and while Didi has not eradicated her fear, she has triumphed over it. Unless someone told you, you'd never know she was a victim. That's because she refuses to think like a victim. Yes, she is more cautious and less daring, but she is, again, a fountain of exuberance — friendly, funny and, most surprisingly, upbeat about life and optimistic about people.

By a daily act of sheer will we have to call courage, she chooses to let the sun shine in. She emerged from her terrible ordeal with a new sense of strength and confidence. She lived through horror and was not destroyed. She found that she could laugh again, trust again and live again. Her knowledge that she could not only survive tragedy but thrive after it is a vaccine against fear. It's a vaccine we can all produce.

Conquering Fear by Facing It

The fear of bodily injury is not unusual. But there are other fears, though less intense, that are even more common. These fears imprison thousands of men and women in unhealthy, dysfunctional and even abusive personal and work-related relationships.

First is fear of change and uncertainty. Believing that "the devil you know is better than the devil you don't," people infected with this fear think bad relationships and jobs are better than nothing and their self-image is so low they can't imagine something better coming along.

Second is fear of disapproval. Some people dread embarrassment or rejection so much they are unwilling to do anything that risks the disapproval of others.

Third is fear of failure. Many people are so frightened by the possibility of failure they accept whatever they have as enough.

Last is fear of financial insecurity. Some people worry so much about how they will survive financially that they chain themselves to unhappy situations.

The common thread is an abiding but false feeling of inadequacy concerning the ability to handle challenges. There is no chemical antidote to fear and it's usually futile to lecture fearful people about replacing apprehension with self-assurance. We can't change timidity to boldness by edict or exhortation, but there is a strategy that can work. We can't simply manufacture courage and confidence, but we can force ourselves to act courageously even in the face of fear.

Don't wait to feel unafraid or certain. Think of yourself as an actor and act the way a brave person would. Fake it if you have to, but get moving! Each time you look fear in the face you gain power over fear. And whether you believe it or not, you will survive — and in taking over your life, you will eventually thrive.

Michael Josephson

To subscribe to a free e-mail newsletter of Mr. Josephson's commentaries, please send an e-mail (with "subscribe" in the subject line) to commentary@jiethics.org. For an archive of recent commentaries, please visit www.charactercounts.org.

Joseph and Edna
Josephson Institute of Ethics

The mission of the nonprofit, nonpartisan Joseph and Edna Josephson Institute of Ethics is to improve the ethical quality of society by changing personal and organizational decision making and behavior. Nationally active and based in southern California, the Institute uses presentations, consulting, community trainings, workshops and publications to help focus the moral energy of people who want to do something to make our society more honest, fair, caring and accountable.

The Josephson Institute is not a think tank. Instead, it teaches and encourages people to make principled decisions and carefully consider the effects of their choices. The Institute holds that ethical obligations are based on common values applicable and knowable to all, regardless of gender, race, age, wealth, class, politics or religion. These values, called the Six Pillars of Character, are: trustworthiness, respect, responsibility, fairness, caring and citizenship.

Since 1987 the Institute has conducted programs for more than 100,000 leaders — in government and the armed forces, in business and journalism, in law and law enforcement, and in education and the nonprofit community. The nationwide **CHARACTER COUNTS!** youth initiative and the Pursuing Victory With Honor sportsmanship campaign are projects of the Institute.

Former law professor and businessman Michael Josephson founded the Institute in the name of his parents and serves as its president on a volunteer basis. Often featured in the news media, Mr. Josephson has become one of the nation's most sought-after ethicists. The Institute is overseen by a volunteer, independent board of governors. Mr. Josephson serves as Institute president without salary.

The Institute is a 501(c)(3) nonprofit, tax-exempt organization funded by revenue from its members, programs, products and publications as well as by gifts and grants.

The Institute seeks to:
- Stimulate moral ambition
- Heighten the ability to perceive the ethical dimension of choices
- Teach how to formulate optimal ethical responses
- Show how to implement these responses intelligently

The Institute seeks to enhance the ethical quality of organizational conduct by inspiring leaders to:
- Identify the ethical obligations arising from positions of authority
- Consider the impact of all institutional actions on all stakeholders
- Create workplaces that reward the ethical and discourage the unethical

The Power of Character

Prominent Americans Talk About Life, Family, Work, Values and More

Michael S. Josephson
and Wes Hanson, Editors

There is no higher praise we can give people than to say they have good "character." But what, really, does that mean? What makes this quality so essential to achieving personal success and fulfillment? More important, how can we build our own character and live more satisfying lives? In this unique collection of essays, over 40 distinguished Americans share their perspectives on the meaning of character in family, life, community and work.

Reflecting society's diversity, the authors speak from various cultural and professional backgrounds about living with integrity, honesty and compassion. This select group includes best-selling authors, educators, journalists, artists, business executives, political leaders, attorneys and media figures. From Dan Rather of CBS, radio host Dr. Laura Schlessinger and author Arianna Huffington to management expert Stephen R. Covey, attorney Alan M. Dershowitz and sports commentator John Naber, the contributors explore how character and ethics shape our destinies. They call for the cultivation of character — in ourselves, our co-workers, our neighbors and our children. Their stories are illuminating and will inspire readers to examine character as a means of building better personal lives, and a better world.

CONTRIBUTORS:

Robb Armstrong
Warren Bennis
B. David Brooks
Stephen L. Carter
Martin J. Chavez
Sen. Max Cleland
Charles Colson
Stephen R. Covey
Alan M. Dershowitz
Sen. Pete V. Domenici
Rabbi Wayne Dosick
Susan Estrich
Greg Evans
Linda and Richard M. Eyre

Daniel Goleman
Colin Greer
Vartan Gregorian
Lloyd V. Hackley
Arianna Huffington
Gov. Jane Dee Hull
Michael S. Josephson
Rushworth M. Kidder
Elizabeth Kiss
Ralph S. Larsen
Adm. Charles R. Larson
Thomas Lickona
Oseola McCarty
Sanford N. McDonnell

Ann Medlock
Sylvester Monroe
John Naber
Dennis Prager
Dan Rather
Rabbi Steven Carr Reuben
Dr. Laura Schlessinger
Rev. Robert H. Schuller
Christina Hoff Sommers
Rabbi Joseph Telushkin
Brig. Gen. Malham M. Wakin
Marianne Williamson
Edward A. Wynne

Parenting to Build Character in Your Teen

By Michael S. Josephson,
Val J. Peter and Tom Dowd

Building character in teens is a matter of teaching them to "know the good, love the good, and do the good." In this book, two of America's foremost youth-serving organizations, the **CHARACTER COUNTS!** Coalition and Girls and Boys Town, team up to help parents accomplish this vital task.

Learn how to use proven Common Sense Parenting® techniques to teach, enforce, advocate and model the Six Pillars of Character — trustworthiness, respect, responsibility, fairness, caring and citizenship. This book will show you as a parent how to help an adolescent build character using his or her:

■   **HEAD** – Teach right from wrong and help your teen understand the importance of good behavior and each of the Six Pillars of Character.

■   **HEART** – Help him or her develop a strong conscience and commitment to values like honesty, courtesy and dependability.

■   **HABITS** – Reinforce good behavior and attitudes so that they become a permanent part of your teen's life.

Also included . . . A seven-step ethical decision-making process for teens and tips for parents on helping teens deal with pressures to have sex, temptations to shoplift or cheat, and threats from bullies.

Looking for Good Ideas to Teach Young People?

As the popularity of character education grows, the need for new teaching ideas increases. The *Good Ideas* book is a cornucopia of lesson plans and activity ideas organized by five age groups (from four-year-olds to teenagers) and by ethical value. Many of the ideas were submitted by hard-working, creative teachers in schools across the country; other ideas were developed by the editors from a variety of sources. This newest collection combines the lesson plans of volumes one and two into a single convenient, lively and cost-effective volume.

In addition to over 200 classroom activities, the new edition features an updated front-of-the-book resources section, which includes:

- stories about what communities around the country are doing to promote character education
- community- and school-wide activities
- lists of useful Internet resources
- pointers for parents
- tips for involving the business community
- ideas for garnering local political support
- suggestions for raising awareness
- tips on arranging speaking engagements
- sample documents: a press release, a speech, public service announcements and various letters to prospective supporters
- and more!